BABY-SITTERS LITTLE SISTER®

KAREN'S GRANDMOTHERS

DON'T MISS THE OTHER BABY-SITTERS LITTLE SISTER GRAPHIC NOVELS!

KAREN'S WITCH

KAREN'S ROLLER SKATES

KAREN'S WORST DAY

KAREN'S KITTYCAT CLUB

KAREN'S SCHOOL PICTURE

KAREN'S BIRTHDAY

KAREN'S HAIRCUT

KAREN'S SLEEPOVER

ANN M. MARTIN

BABY-SITTERS LITTLE SISTER®

KAREN'S GRANDMOTHERS

A GRAPHIC NOVEL BY

DK YINGST

WITH COLOR BY BRADEN LAMB

An Imprint of
SCHOLASTIC

This book is for Bethany Buck, who helps make Karen come alive
A. M. M.

This book is dedicated to my mom and dad. Congratulations on the birth of your first grandchild, my niece, Eloise Rose
D. Y.

Library of Congress Control Number: 2023947635

ISBN 978-93- 5954- 594- 3
This reprint edition : July 2025
Printed at Acme Print o Pac Pvt.Ltd. Noida

Edited by Cassandra Pelham Fulton
Creative Director: Phil Falco
Publisher: David Saylor

CHAPTER 1

It's so hot today! We should start school in October when it's cooler and not in September.

Then we'd have to go to school until July to make up for it.
Aa Bb Cc
Ms. Colman
Today:

Oh yeah, you're right.
I like Ricky and he likes me.

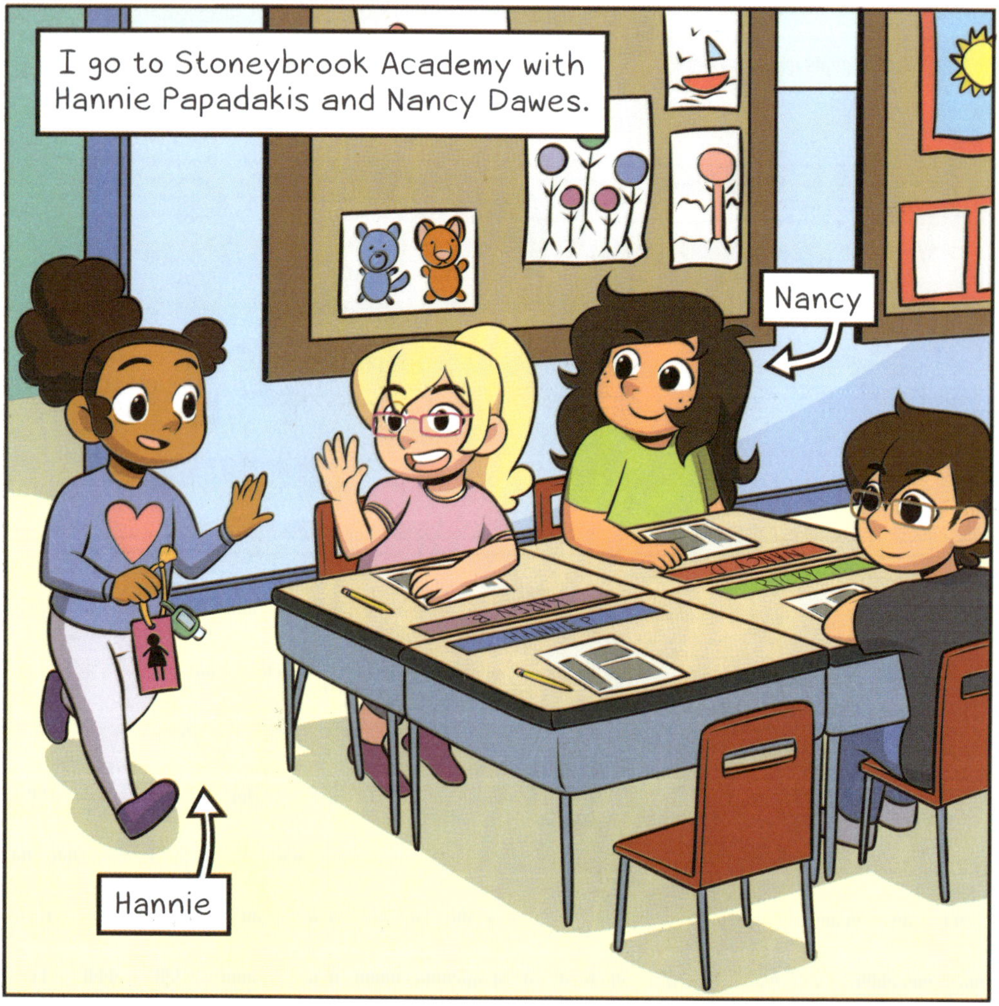

I go to Stoneybrook Academy with Hannie Papadakis and Nancy Dawes.

Nancy

Hannie

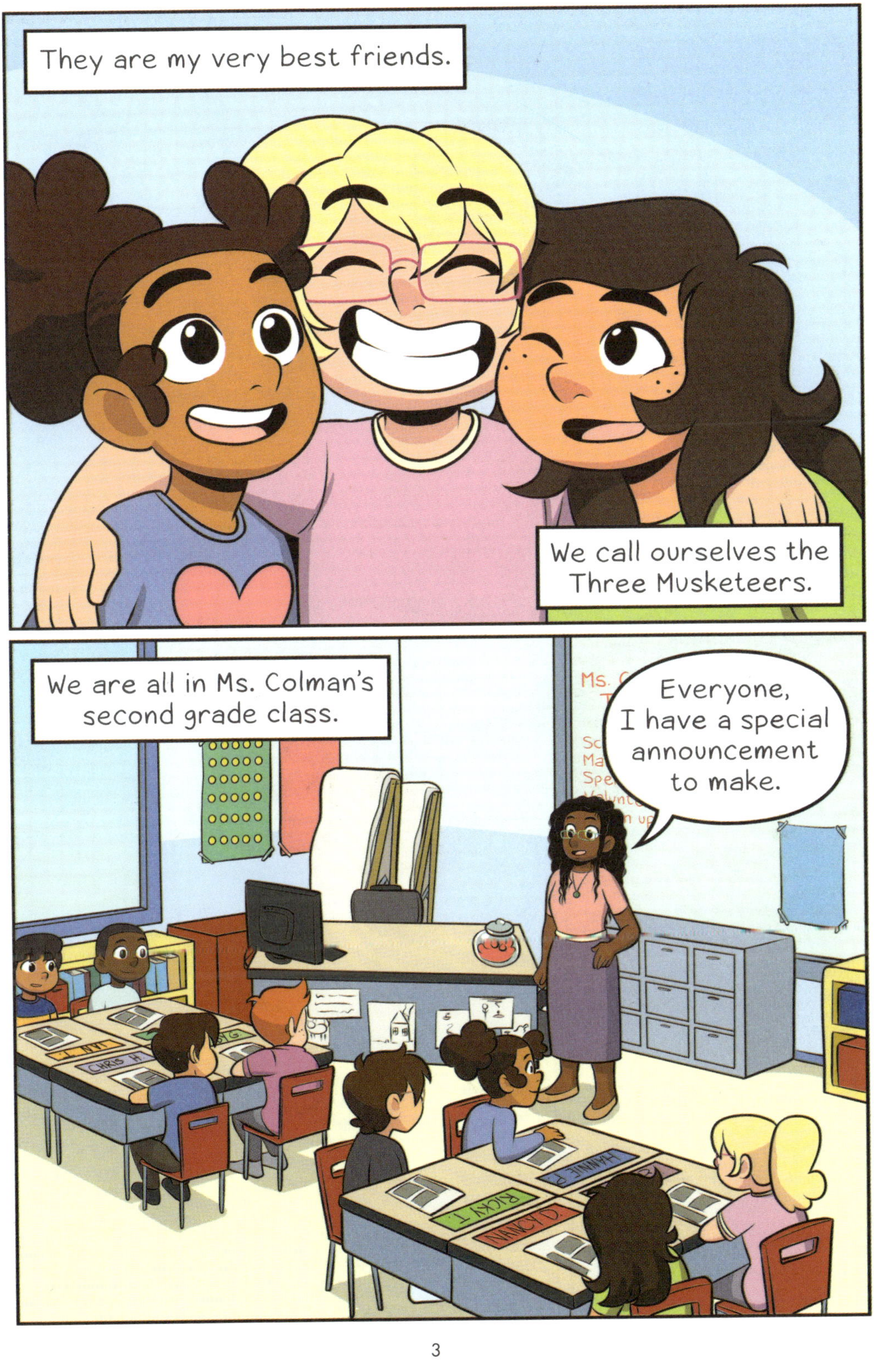

They are my very best friends.

We call ourselves the Three Musketeers.

We are all in Ms. Colman's second grade class.

Everyone, I have a special announcement to make.

How many of you have heard of the Adopt-a-Grandparent program?
Adopt A Grandparent

SARA F.
NATALIE S.
SHAWN J.

Okay...how many of you know what Stoneybrook Manor is?

Karen?

Stoneybrook Manor is where older people live when they need help taking care of themselves.
That's right.

Ms. Colman
Today:
Science
Math
We've been chosen to "adopt" some of the people there.

Our class has been given a special honor. Anyone who is interested will be assigned to a resident.
KAREN B.
HANNIE P
RICKY T.
You'll visit your new "grandparent" twice a week after school.

Science
It will mean a lot to the people there. Some of them don't get many visitors.
Adopt
A
randparent

Who would like to adopt a grandparent?
I would!
Me!!
Here's the thing. My parents got divorced, and then they each got married again.

That means I have four grandmothers -- two regular ones and two stepgrandmothers.

If I adopt a fifth grandma, I'll set a new grandmother record!

If you would like to talk about this with your friends, I will give you till the end of class to do that.
You may leave your seats.

Nancy, don't you want to adopt a grandmother or grandfather?

You don't have any of your own.
Nope.

But grandparents are great. They like to give stuff to kids.
Adopting a grandparent will be fun! Besides, some of the people in the home are really lonely.

They need --
No, thank you.

. . . .

Adopt A
A bus will take you to the manor and then pick you up each time you visit.
BOBBY G.
OMAR H.

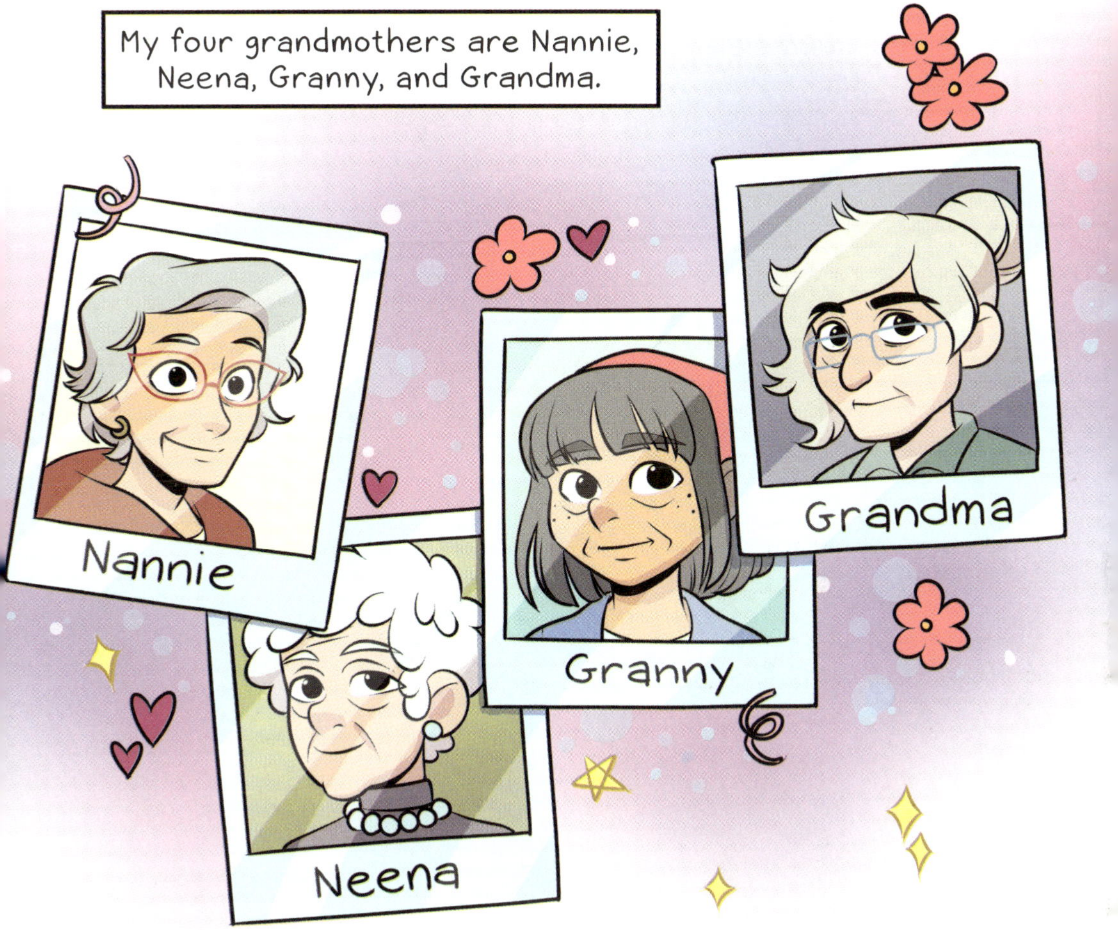

My four grandmothers are Nannie, Neena, Granny, and Grandma.

Nannie

Neena

Granny

Grandma

When Mommy got married again, she married Seth.
He is my stepfather.
Granny is Seth's mother.
She lives on a farm in Nebraska, which is far, far away.
When Daddy got married again, he married Elizabeth.
She is my stepmother.
And Nannie is her mother.

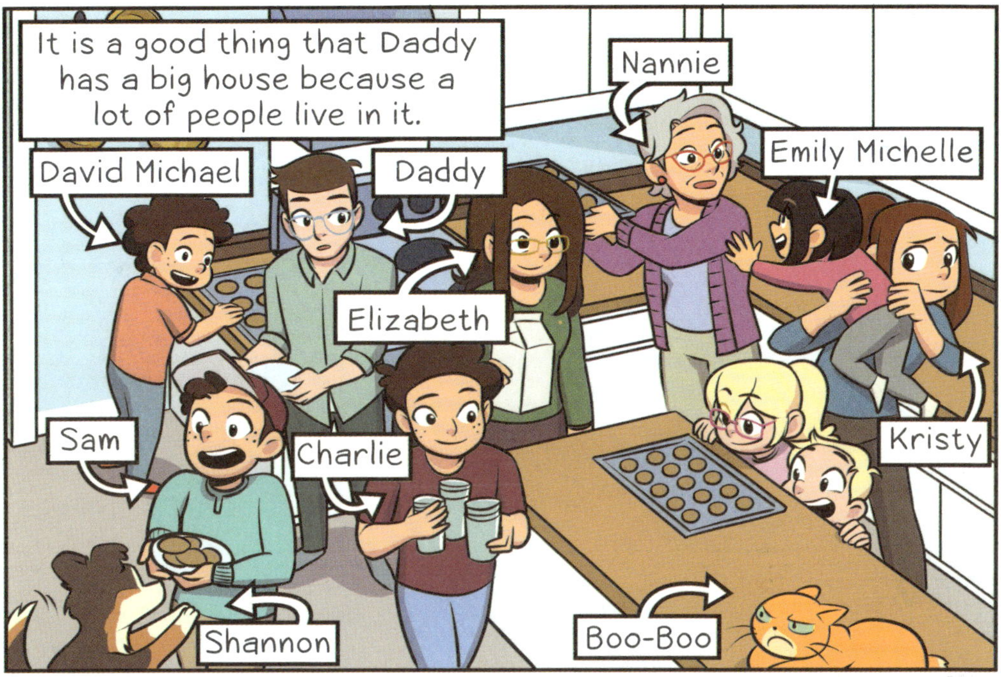

It is a good thing that Daddy has a big house because a lot of people live in it.

Nannie

David Michael

Daddy

Emily Michelle

Elizabeth

Sam

Charlie

Kristy

Shannon

Boo-Boo

Mommy and Seth live in the little house.
Mommy
Seth
Emily Junior
Rocky
Midgie

Andrew is my little brother.
He's four, going on five.

We mostly live at Mommy's house. But every other weekend we live at Daddy's.

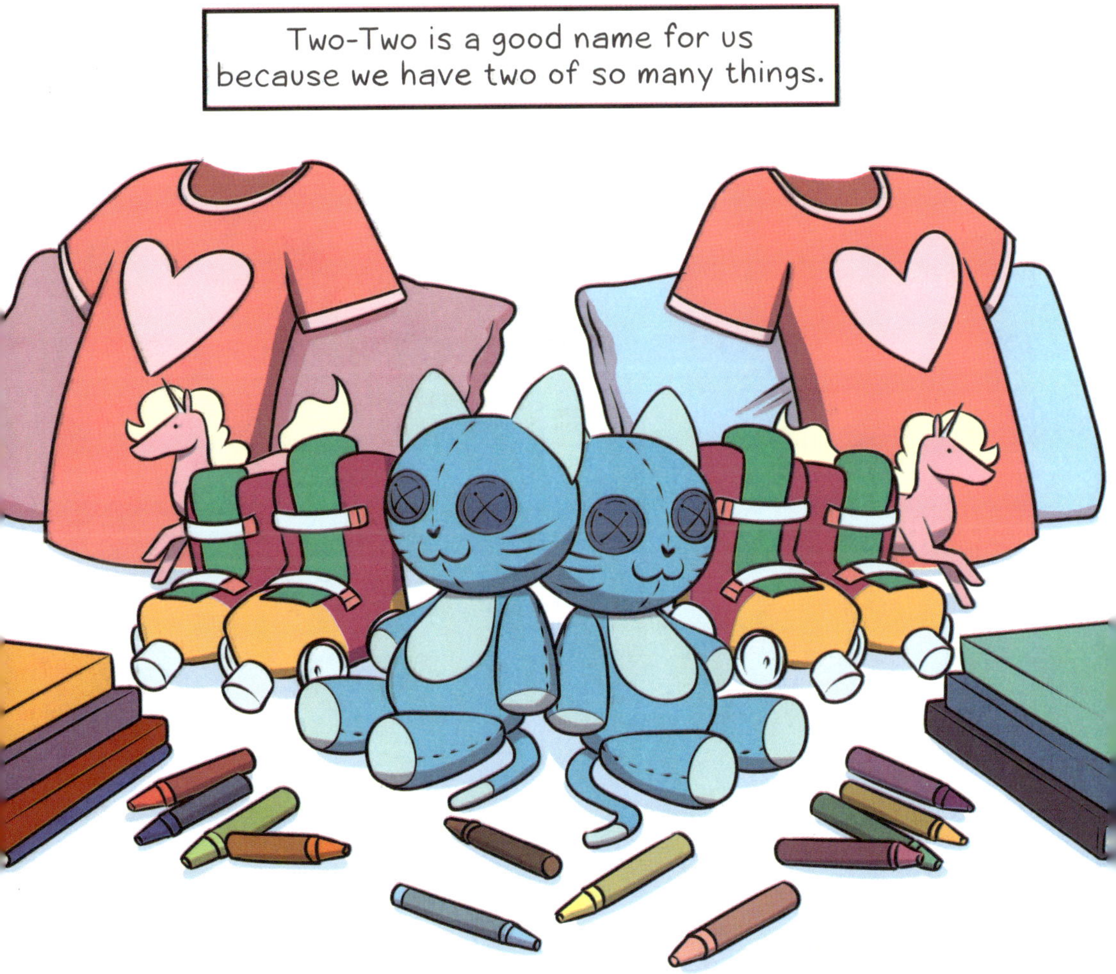

Two-Two is a good name for us because we have two of so many things.

I even have two best friends.
Nancy lives next door to the little house...

And Hannie lives across the street from the big house.

I don't have two of everything, though. Sometimes being a two-two is fun.

Sometimes it is not so much fun.
RIIIP!
Half for each house

But I do like having four grandmas.

That is super special.

And if I could have a fifth, that would be even better.
I do not know anybody with five grandmas.

CHAPTER 2

Nancy does not have any brothers or sisters, just her mom and dad.

That is why I want her to adopt a grandparent, so she'll have a bigger family.

Thank you, Mrs. Dawes!
Bye, Nancy!
Bye, Karen.

Hi, honey!

Here. I am going to adopt a grandparent!
Most Grandmas EVER
If it is a grandmother, then I will have five grandmas. That would be so cool!
See? We will go to Stoneybrook Manor two times a week.
Two afternoons a week?
Yes. This is a special honor for the kids in Ms. Colman's class.
But, Karen, you are already very busy.
You take art lessons on Wednesdays...
You like to meet with your Fun Club, and sometimes you practice with the Krushers, too.
The Krushers are a softball team that Kristy coaches.

I know, but I really, really, really want to adopt a grandparent. Especially a grandma.
Even though you'll be busy two more afternoons each week?
Yes.
Stoneybrook Manor Permission Slip
Student: Karen Brewer
Parent: Lisa
Well, all right...

Oh, thank you!!
I'm going over to Nancy's now!
Be home before dinner!
I will!

Mommy signed my slip!

Good for you.

What's wrong?
I don't know.

I think you need a grandma or grandpa.

No! I do not need one!

Why? Why won't you go to Stoneybrook Manor with me?

Because...

I am afraid of old people.

I don't have any grandparents. Sometimes I wish I did.
What?

But most times, I think I would be afraid of them.
You are not afraid of Nannie.

Nannie does not seem like an old person.
She goes bowling. She drives a car. She doesn't even look old. I am afraid of really old people, and most grandparents are really old.

Why do old people scare you?
I don't know...

I need to do something to help Nancy.

And I'm getting an idea.

How do I show Nancy that “old” does not mean “bad” or “scary”?

Older people are just people, except they might have wrinkles or white hair, or no hair at all.

Some of them can’t walk as fast as younger people.
They might even need help getting around. But those are not reasons to be afraid of them.

Young people can have different color hair, too. Sometimes they dye it. And babies can't walk at all!
I wish I could find a grandparent for Nancy.
That's it, Goosie! We're going to find one for Nancy.
Now, who could I get?
Nannie? No, she is too busy.
Maybe one of my other grandmas? After all, I have four, and maybe five. I can certainly share one with a friend.

I can write to Granny in Nebraska. Maybe she could be Nancy's pen-pal grandmother!

And if she got some special mail, she would feel almost like she really does have a grandma.
This is perfect. Nancy can have a grandma, and she will not feel afraid.

What should I write, Goosie?
xxx kisses ~from Karen ~

My friend Nancy is very
nice and she loves to act.
I think she might be an
actress one day.

I think
actress one

I think Nancy needs a
grandma. And I am
wondering if you would be
her pen-pal grandma.

randma. And I am
ondering if you wo
er pen-pal grandr

I would like to be a
pen-pal grandma.

☐ Yes

☐ No

CHAPTER 3

It is a big day! We are going to see our adopted grandparents for the first time.

I have butterflies in my stomach.

What do you think our adopted grandparents will be like?

Old.

Ricky is funny. I feel a little less nervous now.

I feel very proud of myself.
I, Karen Brewer, am going to help someone.
RECORD BREAKER
#1 Granddaughter
Most
And maybe I will set a new grandmother record!

Don't be
afraid.

Stoneybr
Manor

Look at all the little tots!

Ooh, I'm glad Nancy isn't here.

Hello, I am Mrs. Fellows. Thank you for coming to volunteer. Please follow me.

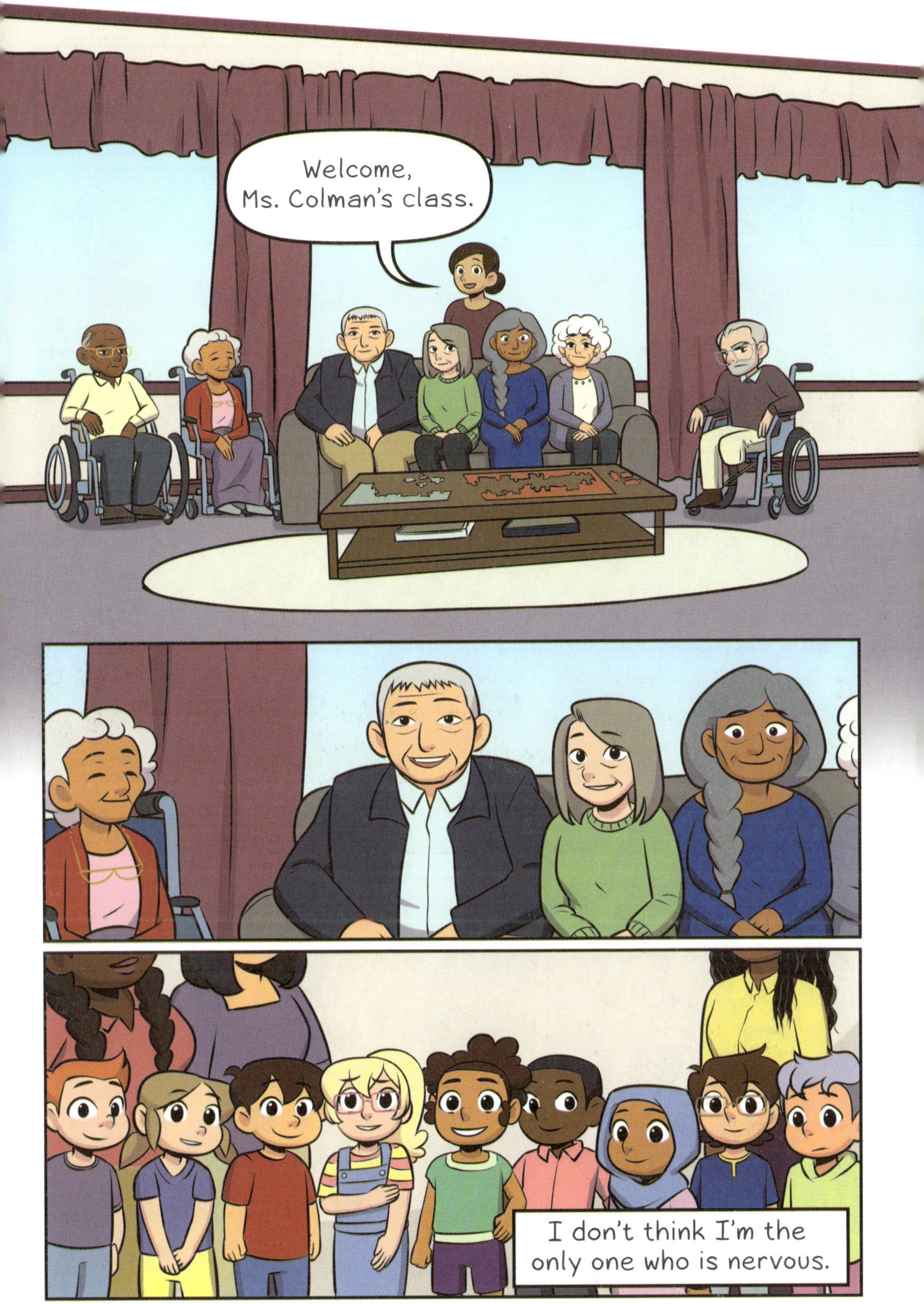

Welcome,
Ms. Colman's class.

I know you are eager to meet your new grandparents,
So I will read each of your names and the names of your adopted grandparents.
Then you can get acquainted.

Oh, please, please, please let me have another grandmother!

Bobby and Mrs. Lee. Jannie and Mr. Danny...

Karen Brewer and Esther Barnard.

Esther!

Hi! I'm Karen, and you are Esther Barnard. Guess what. You are my fifth grandmother!
My goodness!

Guess what else. I have a brother, three stepbrothers, a stepsister, and a baby sister.
Do you have a family?

Yes, but they live in Chicago. I have two daughters and six grandchildren. Four boys and twin girls.
Twins!

Do you want to see some pictures?

This is my eldest and her three boys...
And my sons-in-law on their annual fishing trip.
Oh! And this is my favorite picture of the twins.
So precious.

Okay, children, our hour is over. It's time to go.

What should I call you?

How about Grandma B?

Perfect! And you can call me Karen.

Guess what!
Indoor voice.

Guess what. I have five grandmas now.

My new grandma is named Esther Barnard, but I will call her Grandma B.

Sounds like you had fun volunteering.
You got some mail today, Karen.

Mail? For me? Where is it?
On the kitchen table.

I usually only get mail on my birthday.

It must be from Granny.
Karen Brewer
12 Forest Drive
Stoneybrook CT 06800

Oh boy!
Dear Granny,
How are you?
Andrew & I are fine
like this paper.
for giving it to me.
My friend Nancy is very
nice and she loves to act.
I think she might be an
actress one day.
I think Nancy needs a
grandma. And I am
wondering if you would be
her pen-pal grandma.
I would like to be a
pen-pal grandma.
Yes
No

flip
Nancy Dawes

Dear Karen,
It was so nice to hear from you. Thank you for writing! ♡

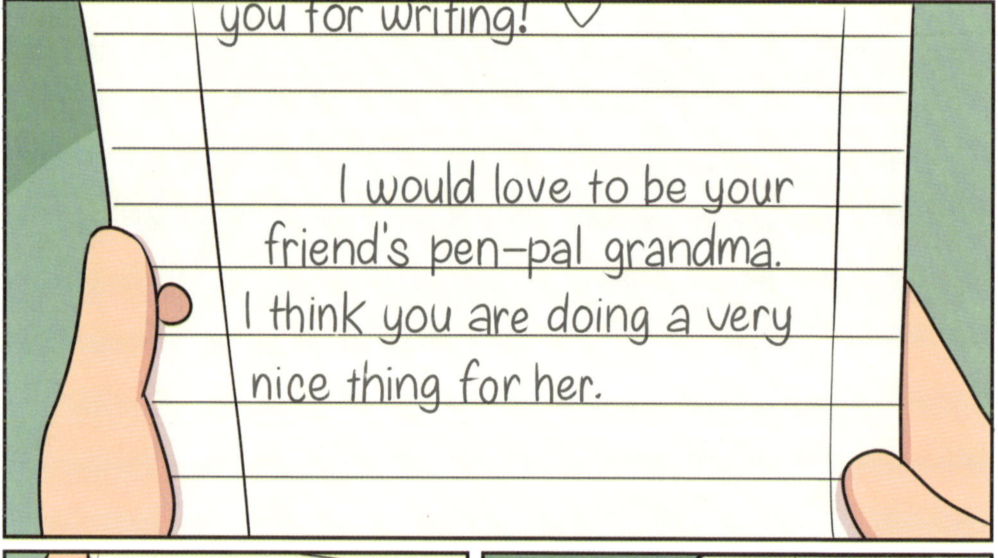
you for writing! ♡
I would love to be your friend's pen-pal grandma. I think you are doing a very nice thing for her.

So I am sending her a letter. You can take it to her and explain who it is from.
Love,
Granny

My idea worked! I have to get to Nancy's house right away.

Granny must have sent Nancy more than just a letter.

Hmm...
I wonder what it is.
Nancy Dawes
Karen Brewer
12 Forest Drive
oneybrook CT 06800

There is only one way to find out!

Guess what.
What?

You have a grandmother now!
Nancy Dawes

I have a grandmother?
Yes. I asked my grandma who lives in Nebraska if she would be your pen-pal grandma, and she said yes!
Nancy Dawes

Here's your first letter from Granny. I think she sent you something else, too.
Nancy Dawes

I didn't get any photos.

Wow, I like getting mail.

Gosh, your grandmother sounds great, Karen. She says she feeds the chickens every day. And sometimes she rides a tractor!

Will you write back to her?
Well...sure.
I guess I have to. But it will be fun.

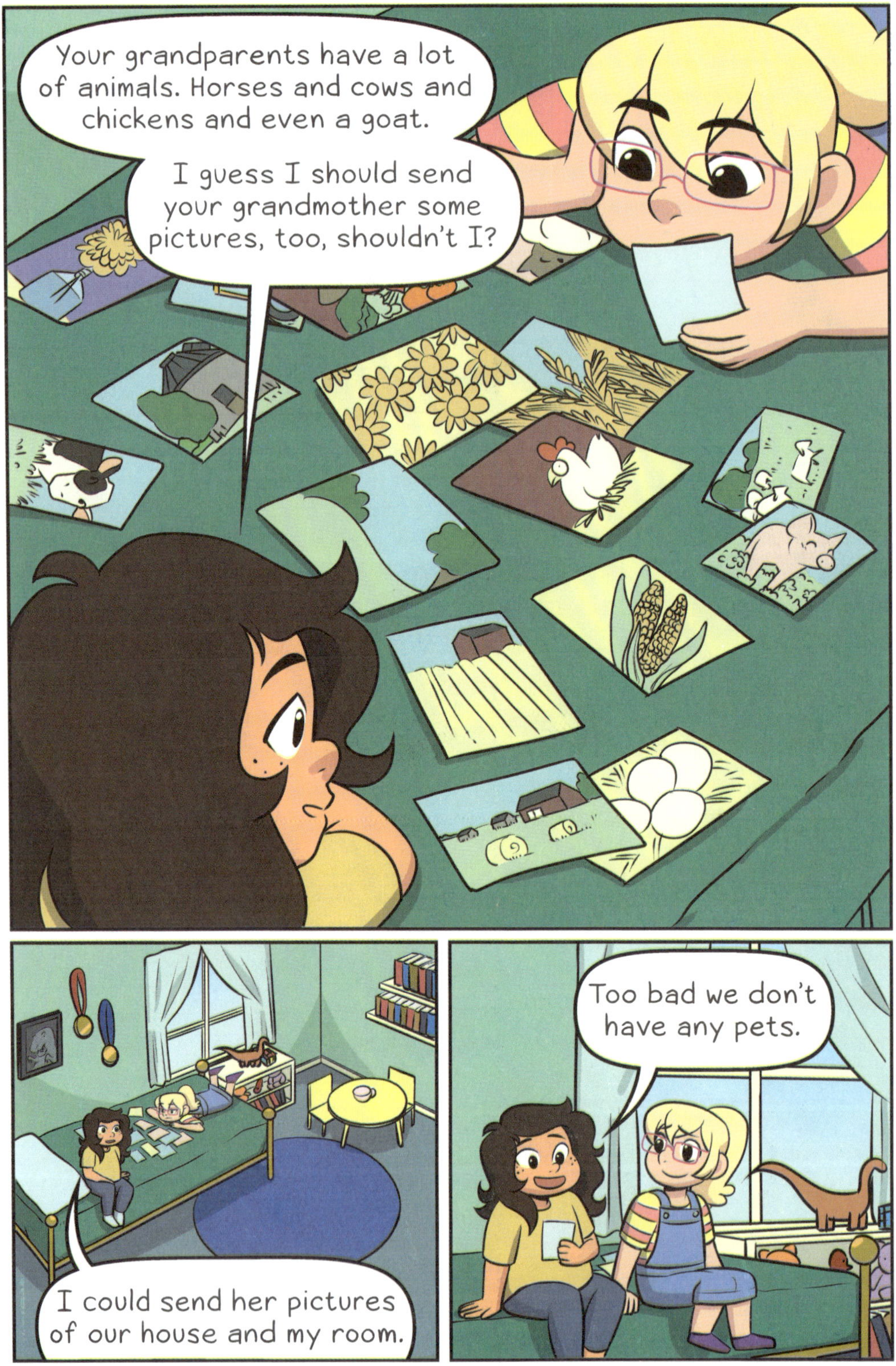

Your grandparents have a lot of animals. Horses and cows and chickens and even a goat.
I guess I should send your grandmother some pictures, too, shouldn't I?

I'm glad my idea worked. I did something nice for both Granny and Nancy.

Why didn't Granny send **me** any pictures?

Oh well. At least Nancy is happy.

Maybe I should send Granny some pictures, too. And while I'm at it, I can take some pictures to show Grandma B.

Yeah, that is a good idea.

CHAPTER 4

It has been two weeks, and I have visited Grandma B four times.
I took pictures of Mommy and Daddy and Andrew and brought them to Stoneybrook Manor to show her.
While I was at it, I sent copies of the pictures to Granny in Nebraska.

Class, I have an announcement to make.
HANNIE P.
KAREN
RICKY T.
NANCY D.

You may put your books away now so you can listen.

Ms. Colman looks more excited than ususal.

My announcement is that our class is going to give all the people at Stoneybrook Manor a special Grandparents' Day.

Goody!
KAREN
HANNIE P.
NANCY D.
RICKY T.

Grandparents' Day can be whatever we make it. I thought we could put on a program and make a gift for every person staying at the manor.

Yes, Karen?
What kind of program would we put on?

Whatever you want. Some variety might be nice. Maybe a skit, some songs, some poetry. Let's all break into groups.

Each group can plan one part of the program. The important thing is that everyone in this class must participate.

If you are shy about being in the program, you do not have to sing or act.
But you can still help make presents, come to Stoneybrook Manor to pass them out, and say hello to the people there.

Will we be graded?

Graded? Yes. This is part of your participation grade. Everyone must be part of the project.

Please think about what we could do in our program, what you'd like your role to be, and what kinds of gifts we could make.
Remember that we have to make a lot of them.

Oh boy. I can't wait to be in the program.

Maybe we could put on a play about superheroes.

I would like to be Super Ricky and carry a sword.

NANCY D
RICKY T
KAREN B
HANNIE P
I just want to be the star of some play.

Stoneybrook Academy

Here is your chance to be an actress! You can be in a play on Grandparents' Day.

I want to be the star, though.

No! I am not going to Stoneybrook Manor.

No one can make me go there!

But this is a class project.
I don't care. I'm not going in that place.

Not even to meet Grandma B?
Not even to meet Grandma B.
I guess I will just have to be sick on Grandparents' Day.

-SIGH-

I have discovered something.
I am getting a little tired of Grandma B.

Everyone should appreciate classical music...

Karen, you must learn how to do the waltz...

Oh, look! I just love this one...
I know that is not a nice thing to say, but it is true.

I wish Grandma B liked arts and crafts.
Or reading stories.
Or, better yet, making up stories.
So I am just a little tired of visiting my newest grandma.

-RIIING-
I'LL GET IT!
Indoor voice.
Sorry.

Hello?
Hi, Karen. It's me, Kristy.
Hi, Kristy!

Listen, I'm calling a Krushers practice for tomorrow. Can you come?

I'm supposed to visit Grandma B tomorrow...but I really don't want to listen to any more violin music. And I am tired of waltzing and doing the foxtrot.

Sure, I can come.

Great! Thanks, Karen. See you then.

Mommy, I have Krushers practice tomorrow with Kristy.

You'll have to call Grandma B and tell her you can't visit.
Okay...

I'm really sorry, but I have to practice with my softball team tomorrow.

Good luck, Karen! Play well.

Let's go, Andrew!

Ooooohhhh...

Maybe Grandma B brought me good luck. I played really well.

Mommy, did you see that? I hit the ball out of the park!

Hi, Nancy.
Hi! Guess what! Big news!

CHAPTER 5

Big news? What is it?

It's this! Come on, Karen. Let's go up to your room.
Nancy Dawes
10 Forest Drive
Stoneybrook CT 06800

Okay, **now** tell me your big news...and what is **that?**

This is a letter from your grandmother in Nebraska. From my new pen-pal grandma!
You mean you wrote to her and she wrote back?
Yep.

Hmm. Granny hasn't answered my letter yet.

That isn't all. She sent me a pair of mittens with my name on them! She knitted them herself!
NANCY
NANCY

Really?
Boy. I can't believe it.

Granny knitted me a pair of mittens with my name on them last year. I had thought my Karen-mittens were very special.
KAREN

You want to see what's in the letter?
Sure.
But I guess Granny knits name-mittens for any girl who comes along.

Okay, well, the letter is three pages long. And your grandma sent more pictures!
Here is one of the barn cats and her kittens.
There are five kittens.
And two of them look like Pearl.
Pearl is the barn cat.
I know who Pearl is.
And here is a picture of your grandfather's new plow.
And this is the new decoration on the front door of the house.
And this is Spinky.
Hmmm.
Karen?
Yeah?

In her letter, your grandmother said I should decide what to call her. She thinks "Pen-Pal Grandma" is too long.
I can't call her Mrs. Engle. Not if she's sort of my grandmother.

And I can't call her Granny, because that's what you and Andrew call her. So I thought of a new name. I'm going to call her Big Mama.
Do you think she will like it?

It is not fair that Nancy also got name-mittens from Granny and received more letters from her, too.
NANCY
NANCY
I did not want to tell Nancy what I really thought.

Big Mama. Let me see. I think that is a perfect name for Granny.

Start your next letter "Dear Big Mama," and see what happens.
Okay!

Do you want to play with Emily Junior?

No, thank you. I am very busy. I better go. I have to write to Big Mama.

Also, I have decided to make a present for her, since she knitted mittens for me.
I wonder what I should make for her.

I don't know, but tell me what happens when you get a letter back from...Big Mama.
I will!

Today, class, we will start planning our program for Grandparents' Day.

We have a lot of work to do.

I want you to decide what gifts to make, and, if you are going to be in the program, break into groups and decide what you'd like to do.
Grandparents' Day Program
ideas:

Each group should plan something different.
Oh boy. This is going to be so fun!

Who has an idea for gifts that we could make?
Yes, Natalie?

How about pot holders?

Well, that is a nice thought, but the people at the manor do not have to cook.
They eat in a dining room. Any other ideas?

Cakes and cookies?
Another good idea, but a lot of the residents are on special diets. Some of them cannot eat cakes and cookies.

After a lot of talking, we decided to make necklaces and pencil cups for the residents.
Good ideas, everyone. Now you may break into groups of three or four if you want to be in the program.
Cookies
necklaces
bookmarks
pot holders
plants
pencil holders
I wanted to be in the program, of course. So did Hannie. Even Nancy did. She just could not pass up a chance to act in front of an audience.

Guess who else joined our group. Ricky Torres!
How come you want to work with us?

Because I know you are going to put on a play, and I want to be in it. I want to be Super Ricky.

I want to carry a sword.

But, Ricky, we have not decided to put on a play about superheroes.

I think it's a good idea. I could be Super Nancy, and you guys could be Super Karen and Super Hannie.
KAREN B.
HANNIE P.
RICKY T.

Is that what we want to do? A superhero play?

I want to put on a play about a little lost kitten.

Oh, that is boring. That is girl stuff.
But I **am** a girl!
So what?

KAREN B.
NANCY D.
HANNIE P.
RICKY T.
We will have to think about our play some more. It has to be the best part of the program!

CHAPTER 6

I had to miss another visit to Grandma B.
It wasn't my fault, though.

Grandma B... I have an earache and won't be able to come tomorrow.

Feel better soon, Karen. Do everything your mother tells you to do.
I hope you will be able to come next time. I miss you.

I miss you, too.
I do miss Grandma B.

Sort of.

A few days later

Stone
Ma

Hello, hello!

You smell like cherry candy, Grandma B!

Let's go to my room, Karen.
Uh-oh.

No music today?

Karen, it is almost time for the High Holy Days.

The holidays? Not really. Christmas is more than three months away.

I take the High Holy Days very seriously.

Oh, me too.
I'm glad to hear that. I have always observed the ten days of penitence.
Does she mean the twelve days of Christmas?

...Rosh Hashanah...
...Yom Kippur...
I am getting bored.
Sigh

Grandma B, do you know who Connie Cat is?

No, I don't believe I do.

Well, this is Connie. She's from the Isle of Tales, but now lives in England with a nice family, the Browns.

Connie goes on adventures with their cat, Charcoal the artist. He is very talented.

I am glad that Grandma B likes Connie Cat as much as I do.

And that we have stopped talking about High Holidays.

Today is special. It's a going-to-Daddy's-house Friday!

Hey, Karen!

But something else made it even more special. Mommy had given me a letter from Granny that had come in the mail!
Oh boy!

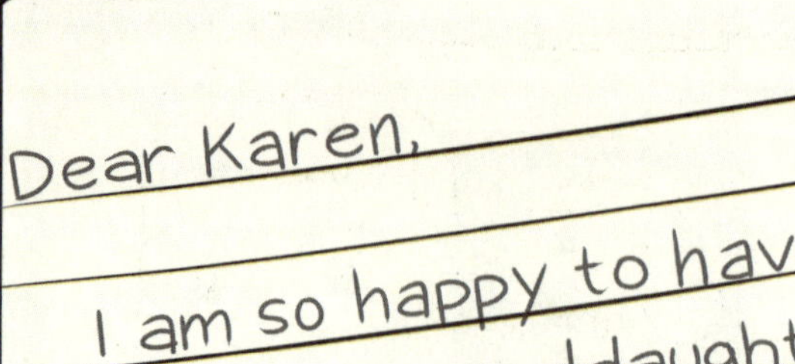
Dear Karen,
I am so happy to have you as my granddaughter and Nancy as my pen-pal granddaughter.

I am really only her stepgranddaughter.

Guess what.
Nancy calls me Big Mama now. Isn't that funny? I just love the name.

Hmm. Granny liked the name "Big Mama"?

She told me about the new tractor and a bunch of stuff I already knew from Nancy's letters.

She did not send any pictures. But she told me she liked the things that Nancy had been sending her. And she didn't say anything about the pictures I sent her.

I did not expect Granny to like Nancy so much.

Granny sounds as if she likes Nancy as much as she likes me. Is that because I am just her stepgranddaughter?

And what about adopted grandchildren? How do grandmas feel about them?

There is only one person to ask. Nannie.

Nannie?

Yes?
You have a lot of grandchildren.

You have Kristy and David Michael and Sam and Charlie, who are your regular grandchildren.

And you have Andrew and me. We are your stepgrandchildren.
And Emily is your adopted grandchild.

That's right, and I love you all.

Just the same?

I love you the same amount, but for different reasons.
And the reasons don't have anything to do with whether you're steps, adopted, or "regular" kids.

She is knitting a sweater for me!
I had helped her choose the colors.

Grandmothers have room in their lives for lots of different kinds of grandchildren.

Thank you, Nannie. I feel much better.

CHAPTER 7

DIIING—
DOONG
I'll get it!

Who is it?
It's me, Hannie.

Hi! I have a great idea. Let's work on our play for Grandparents' Day.
Wouldn't it be great if we went to school on Monday and had a terrific play for our group?
Sure!

Let's go to my room.

I have been thinking. The people at the manor might not understand a play about superheroes.

But Halloween is coming up, and everyone knows about Halloween. So let's put on a scary play.
Okay.

Now, what kind of scary play should we put on? Who will the play be about?
Morbidda Destiny?

Morbidda Destiny is the name I gave to the woman who lives next door to Daddy.

I know she is a witch.

Or how about a play about a ghost and a witch?
We could write one about Ben Brewer, the ghost who haunts the third floor, and Morbidda Destiny.

Or maybe we could put on a play about Ollie the Ghost. You know, the ghost in the books?

Yes! I could be Ollie, and you could be his friend Miss Amelia the bat.
And Ricky could be his friend Pluto the mouse. And Nancy could be Mrs. Lei.

But who would be Mr. Lei?
Ollie lives in the Leis' attic.

Oh. Hmm. I don't know. I guess we don't have enough people for a play about Ollie.

How about **Ghostbusters?**

Would your adopted grandma know who the Ghostbusters are?
I don't know.

I don't know if Grandma B would, either. Let's keep thinking.

Ew! I have red paint all over my fingers!
Can someone please pass the glue?
I need more yarn!

Paint the macaroni pretty colors. You can even put polka dots on it.

To make a pencil cup, take an empty soup can.

Make sure it is washed very well and that there are no sharp edges.

Cut out a piece of wrapping paper and spread glue on the back.

Then wrap the paper around the can. That's all you have to do!

Isn't that easy?

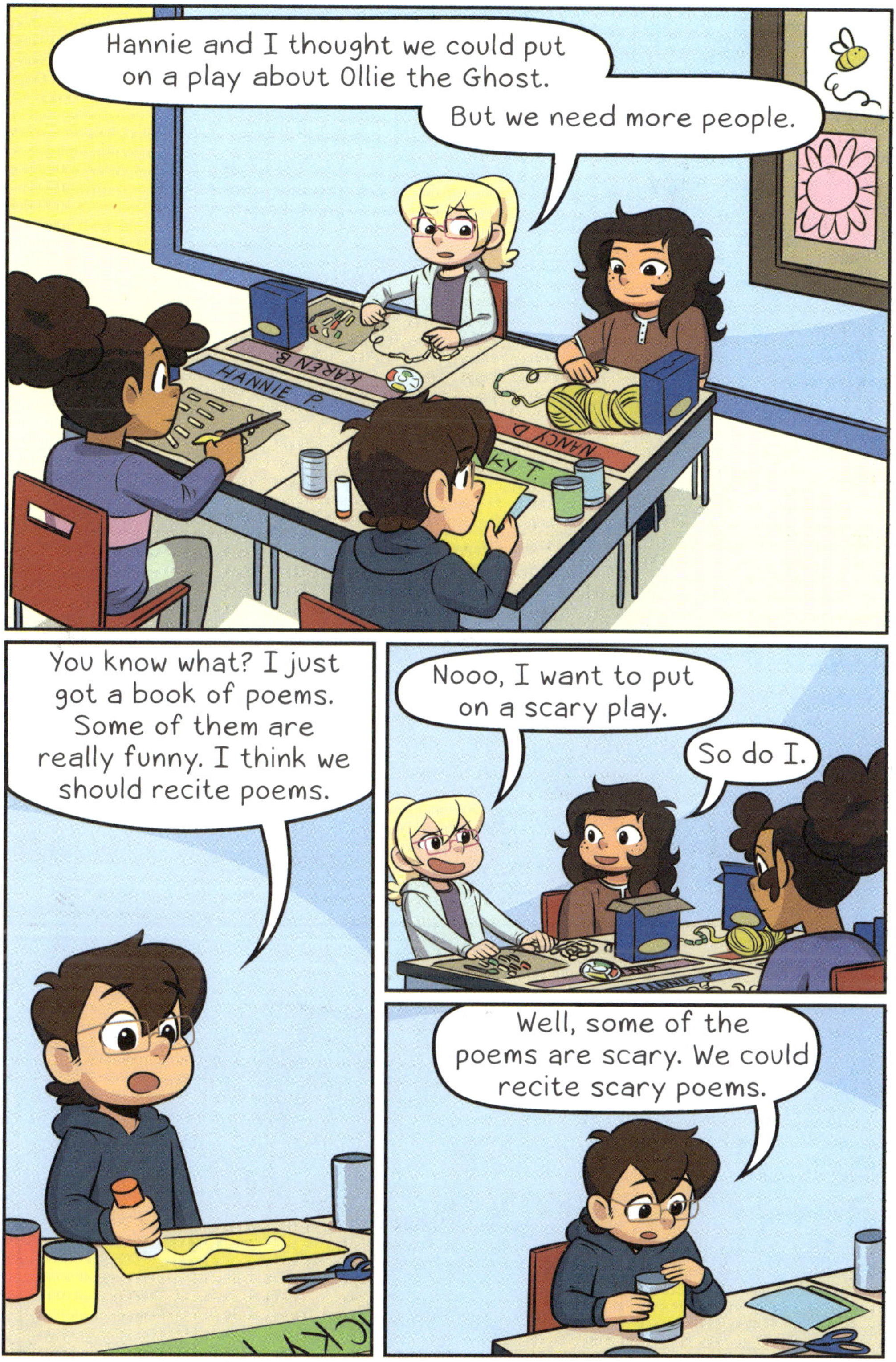

Hannie and I thought we could put on a play about Ollie the Ghost.
But we need more people.

I like that idea. I wanted to be in a play, but reciting poems would be fun.

I guess that idea is okay. Karen?
Maybe. Ricky, what scary poems do you know?

Well, there's a poem in my book called **Some One.**
It is about a person who hears a knock at his door, but when he opens the door, nobody is there.
Knock Knock

Ooh.

I know a scary poem, too. It's about a tree...a strange tree, one that is all twisted and looks at you.
Ew.

Hey! I just thought of a poem that is funny and scary. It's about a little boy whose name is James James Morrison Morrison Weatherby George Dupree.

He is supposed to baby-sit for his mother, only one day his mother says she is going downtown by herself, and after that she is never heard from again.
Isn't that weird?

Yes. Extra weird.

Hannie, do you know any scary poems?
Let me think...

Last year, in first grade, I wrote a poem about Halloween.

Wait a second, is this the one that begins "black cat with a tall, black hat"?
Yes.
NANCY
KAREN B.

Let's stick to grown-up poems.

Fine.

Let's all try to find scary poems, especially poems about Halloween. Then we'll choose some to memorize for the Grandparents' Day program.
KAREN B.
I could hardly wait to go poem hunting.

CHAPTER 8

Ooh, here's a poem about an unlucky black cat.
RIP
RIP
DING-DONG
SOMEONE'S AT THE DOOR!
Andrew, use your indoor voice. You don't have to shout.

I'll get the door. We can read more later!

Nancy Dawes
10 Forest Drive
Stoneybrook CT 06800

Another letter from Granny?

Yes, another letter from Big Mama.

But this one is different. She sent more pictures...

See? They are of herself and...Big Daddy. I guess that is what I should call your grandfather.

What did you think of the photos?

Well, it's funny. Big Mama sounds so young in her letters. She talks about taking care of the animals and working on the farm.

But she looks old in the pictures. Her hair is all gray. And her face has wrinkles. Your grandfather looks old, too.

But see? That's just what I've been trying to tell you.

Lots of grandparents look old, but it does not mean they can't do everyday things like you and me. And some do not even look old, like Nannie.

I know.

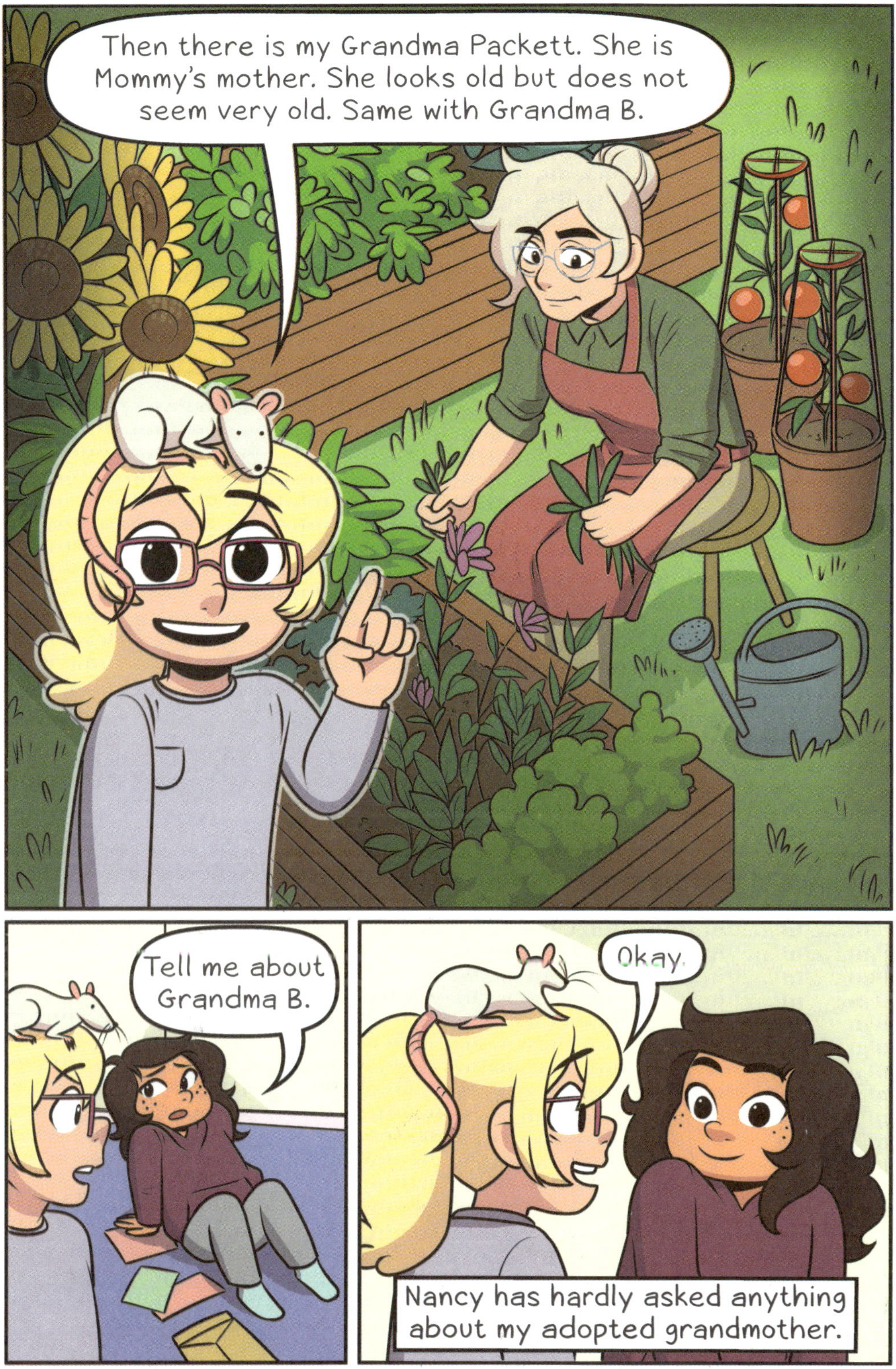

Then there is my Grandma Packett. She is Mommy's mother. She looks old but does not seem very old. Same with Grandma B.

Grandma B...looks pretty old.

As old as Big Mama?
Yes. And she likes to sing and dance.

Dance? I guess that means she gets around okay.

Yes, she does, and you know what one of the nurses at the manor told me?
What?

She told me that Grandma B talks on the phone every evening -- just like a teenager!

I think she talks to her children and grandchildren.
...Maybe Grandparents' Day won't be too bad after all.

I do not think I will mind meeting Grandma B. She sounds okay since she's like Big Mama.

I think she would love to meet you.

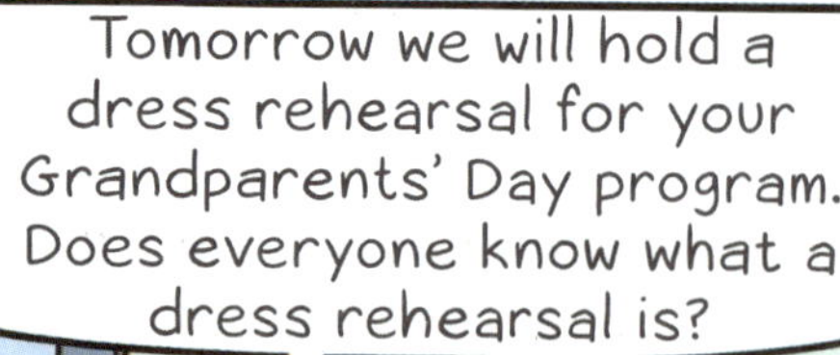

Oh, and another thing. No more reading from scripts. You should have your plays, poems, and songs memorized by now.

BRRIIIINGG

Ricky? Hannie? Nancy? Are we ready for the dress rehearsal tomorrow?

I guess so.

We don't have costumes.
I know, and we haven't memorized our poems yet.

Well, I guess we'll just have to work hard tonight. See you tomorrow!

Dress rehearsal
The first part of the program is a song about pumpkins.

The pumpkin ran away before Thanksgiving day!

SLIP

The pumpkin ran away...
Whoops! Hee hee hee!
Before...umm...
This is not going well.

Now some of the boys are doing the play they wrote.
DINO
DINO
DINO
DINO

They forgot to bring in their props, though.
DINO
DINO

Look! There is a diplodocus!
DINO

This play does not make sense.
HA HA HA HA
HA HA

Thank you, boys.
Group three, it is your turn.

We were each going to recite two short poems.

At first Nancy was going to recite **Strange Trees,** but then she found two other poems she wanted to recite more.
E-F
-J
I can recite **Strange Trees** instead.
Thank you.

Ahem.

Some one strange came knocking at my wee, small door.
Oh no, he's not supposed to say strange...

So I know not who had yellow wrinkles, at all, at all, at all.
That's more mixed up than the beginning.

HA
HA
Hee Hee
HA

We did not recite our own poems much better.

John Jacob Jingleheimer Weatherby George Duschmidt -- uh, I mean James Jamie -- er...hmm.

sigh

Class, our program must be in much better shape before we put it on for the people at the manor.

Your homework tonight is to practice. We will hold another dress rehearsal on Monday.

CHAPTER 9

Mommy! Mommy! Today is Grandparents' Day.

Good morning! You seem excited.

I am very excited. I think I am ready, too. I know both of my poems. Listen to this.

James James Morrison Morrison Weatherby George Dupree took great care of his mother. Though he was only three.

I know the rest, too.
That's wonderful!

And my clothes are laid out.

Is it okay to wear my party shoes to school?
Yes, today is a special occasion.

I just love special occasions!

It's time for our last dress rehearsal.
Everybody looks terrific!
The pumpkin ran away before Thanksgiving day! Said he, you'll make a pie of me if I should stay!
And nothing is going wrong this time.

Some one came knocking at my wee, small door...

James James Morrison Morrison Weatherby George Dupree...

I recite a second poem, one I made up. It's about a girl who lives in a house haunted by a ghost with a witch next door.

The little black cat with the big, tall black hat...
It was much better than Hannie's first-grade poem.

After Nancy's poem, that was it for rehearsal.

And now we are finally going to Stoneybrook Manor!
Stoneybrook Academy

I still do not want
to go to the manor.

We are going to make
the people at the manor
so, so happy.

Yeah, they will like their presents. And they
will love our program. I just know they will.

Can't they love everything
without me there?
Oh, Nancy.

Stoneybrook Manor
Welcome! For all you newcomers, my name is Mrs. Fellows. Thank you for coming. We have all been looking forward to Grandparents' Day.
Please follow me to the all-purpose room.

WOW!

Don't be scared. They are all glad we came.
But that lady over there is asleep.

Well, that's okay. She is probably still glad we came.

A lot of them are like Grandma B. They do not have any family nearby.

Okay, children!

We will put on the program first. Then we will hand out the presents. Please get ready to perform.

Our program is about to begin. We have worked very hard on it. I hope you have fun watching it.

I now present the second grade from Stoneybrook Academy.

I'm so nervous!

Look! There is a diplodocus!

And there is a triceratops. We have found dinosaurs on the moon. We are heroes!

The end!

Okay, here we go.

Some one came knocking at my wee, small door...

James James Morrison Morrison Weatherby George Dupree...

Yay, Karen!
Clap
Clap
Whistle
We haven't made one single mistake.

Great job, everyone! Now we have some refreshments for you. We hope you enjoy!

Yum!

Karen? Nancy? Would you come here, please?

CHAPTER 10

Uh-oh, are we in trouble?

Girls, there are six residents of the manor who are not feeling well and could not come to the program. But we want to give them gifts, too.

I thought it would be nice if they got them from us, and not from a nurse or from Mrs. Fellows later.

Would you please go with Mrs. Fellows to hand out the gifts?
Sure.

Good, thank you.

Ow, Nancy.
Sorry.

Hi. I am Karen and this is Nancy and we have a present for you.

Now come meet Grandma B.

Hi! Grandma B, this is my friend Nancy Dawes. She does not have any grandmas or grandpas, except for a pen-pal grandma.

Hello, Nancy Dawes. How are you?

I'm fine. How are you?

Just fine. I am very excited. I am getting ready for the **High Holy Days.**
Really? Me too!

...Wait a second. I thought Karen said your family lives in Chicago. Are you going to Chicago for Rosh Hashanah and Yom Kippur? Are you staying for Sukkot?

No. But we observe the holidays at the manor. And Mrs. Fellows will probably drive me to temple.

You need a family. Why don't you come to our synagogue with us? And then maybe you can come to our house -- Mommy always makes challah and honey cake and everything!

Do you like to dance?

Oh yes! I am going to be an actress one day. I have to learn to sing and dance and maybe play the piano.

Do you like to listen to music?
Yes, Mommy and Daddy play very beautiful music on our stereo. They say it is classical.

I have just my four regular grandmothers again.
Granny

And now Nancy has an adopted grandma.
Grandma B

Grandma B went to the synagogue with the Daweses for Rosh Hashanah, Yom Kippur, and Sukkot.

Mr. and Mrs. Dawes thought it was nice that Grandma B joined them on the Holy Days.

But they minded that Nancy had invited Grandma B without asking them first.

I have the same rule at my house. First I have to ask Mommy or Seth if I can invite someone over. Then I do the inviting.

She is amazing.

Wow!

She is a gymnast.
Can I be a gymnast?

If you take gymnastics. Do you want to start lessons?

Yes!

Here is the bad thing: I have gymnastics on the days I was supposed to go to Stoneybrook Manor.

Here is the good thing: Now Nancy goes to the manor two times a week.

She is not afraid of the people there anymore.

Well, she's still a little afraid of the grumpiest ones. But that is all.

And she has two grandmas now.
A pen-pal grandma and an adopted grandma.

And Grandma B now has a family in Stoneybrook.
Stoneybrook Manor

Nancy said she has already invited Grandma B over for Hanukkah and Passover Seder.

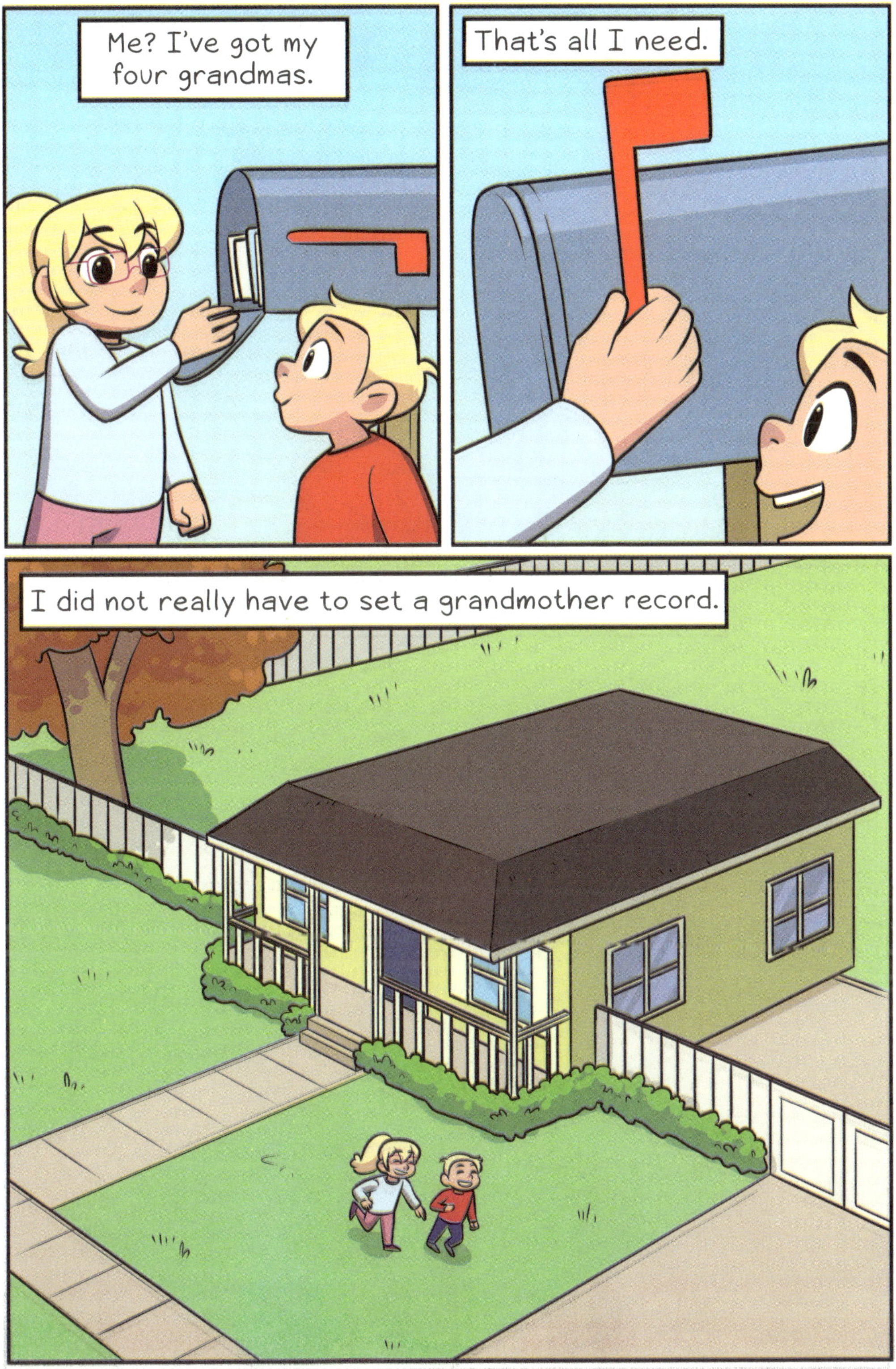

I did not really have to set a grandmother record.

Backward somersault

Shoulder roll

Cartwheel

Roundoff

Hey, Andrew. Watch this!

Ooph!

Was that supposed to happen?
No.

It looks like I will have to practice some more.

Karen! Phone for you. It's Granny from Nebraska.

Goody, goody, goody! I cannot wait to talk to my very own special grandma.

ANN M. MARTIN'S The Baby-sitters Club is one of the most popular series in the history of publishing — with more than 190 million books in print worldwide — and inspired a generation of young readers. Her novels include *Belle Teal*, *A Corner of the Universe* (a Newbery Honor Book), *Here Today*, *A Dog's Life*, and *On Christmas Eve*, as well as the much-loved collaborations *P.S. Longer Letter Later* and *Snail Mail No More* with Paula Danziger, and *The Doll People* and *The Meanest Doll in the World*, written with Laura Godwin and illustrated by Brian Selznick. Ann lives in upstate New York.

DK YINGST is a cartoonist and digital artist from southeast Louisiana. She has an MFA in sequential art from the Savannah College of Art and Design. She loves cute coming-of-age stories, going for meandering hikes, and playing farming sims to relax. She lives in Alabama with her fiancé; their dog, Cookie; and their two cats, Koopa and Connie. Visit her online at dianneyingst.com.

DON'T MISS THE OTHER BABY-SITTERS LITTLE SISTER GRAPHIC NOVELS!

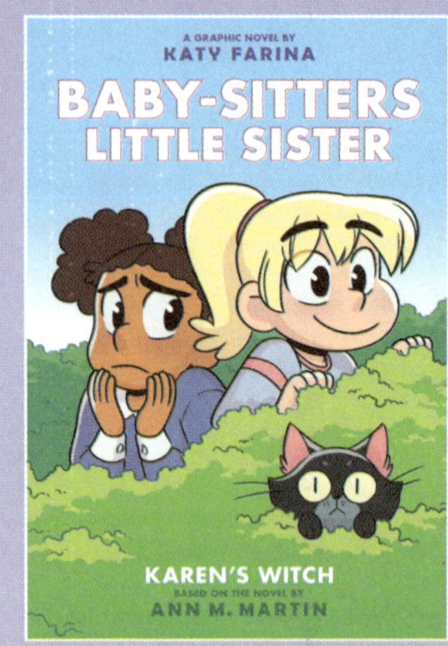